Iaomai ἰά(
Rapha'
Shifa شفاء

The Scroll of Healing

Chahrazade Belamine

Written by Chahrazade Belamine

London, UK, October 2020

PREFACE

I dedicate this book to my family and to those who seek healing and well-being in their lives.

I chose this title 'Iaomai Raphah Shifa, the Scroll of Healing', because those words mean 'Healing' in Greek, Hebrew and Arabic and it creates a link with God and the scriptures.

TABLE OF CONTENTS

Table of Contents

INTRODUCTION

I wrote this book because I felt, that at this moment in time, people are in deep need of healing.

Modernisation, warfare, technology, industrialisation, digital transformation and major events such as Covid19, have had a huge impact on mental health and collective consciousness.

The recent pandemic has created new mindsets, habits and lifestyles whilst growing new ways of communication, interactions and business models. Adapting to the ever-changing world takes strength as the world of technology is constantly evolving. However, the foundation of human soul and mind is still spiritually based.

I found the source of my inner strength in faith and divine grace and I thought it would be helpful to share my experience and knowledge, as many would be able to relate and identify themselves to the challenges described in my book.

I went through the process of identifying all my traumas and struggles and auto-analyse the patterns that I had in my life. And this enabled me to alter my thought process and self-image in order to rebuild into the best version of myself.

CHAPTER I – THE PSYCHE

1– Inner Strength

First, I want to start by saying that life is what you make of it.

Most of the time, the world is a reflection of what we perceive; the total sum of childhood experience, education, environment, beliefs, thoughts and daily life.

And every day you wake up, you get another opportunity to start again, to see the world in a different light. So, in order to make those inner changes, there has to be a level of awareness. And it starts by assessing where you are in life.

One has to stop and ponder.

Who am I?
What are my core values?
What is my ultimate purpose on Earth?

Life has a meaning. The creation of humankind is not random and we all have a role to play in this terrestrial existence.

How could one believe in a spontaneously born universe?

The presence of order, harmony and mathematical precision contradict randomness. The laws of the universe are precise and order and geometry exist in nature. The mere fact that trillions of cells can harmoniously function, grow and develop within the human beings is only one miracle. Notwithstanding the millions of species, the life cycle, the biodiversity, the scaling range from atomic matter to the gigantic scale of the universe, etc. Those are signs of a greater intelligence. And the fact that God's concept is present in the mind indicates its potential reality.

How believing in God is linked to inner strength?

Well, relying on the ultimate source of creation provides meaning, force, substance, vision and energy. And this has always been my core value.

The source of everything and faith is found within.

The results that we have in life are often the reflection of our inner world. When we are aware of this, it becomes the realization of our empowerment. So, inner beliefs impact our outer reality. This is why it is so important to self-assess the areas of your life. I found that the wheel of life is a very practical tool to carry out this assessment and identify which areas need developing and where to put your focus.

The popular saying "Where attention goes, energy flows" makes complete sense.

The wheel of life parameters include:

-Spirituality
-Personal development
-Health and fitness
-Job and career
-Finances
-Couple relationship
-Family and children
-Friends and social life
-Recreation
-Societal contribution

I think that spirituality is the highest point because it links to the infinite, the oneness and a higher realm of consciousness.

When one ponders on those areas of human life, it is easy to see which areas require growth and development.

So, the starting point is always God in the sense that, as spiritual beings, we can reach the realms of soul elevation and consciousness development.

2- The state of the soul

The state of the soul is basically your spiritual connection with the divine.

The Abrahamic scriptures give us an indication of where we come from. A creator that designed spiritual beings to have a human experience on Earth. To that purpose, God has gifted each one of us with abilities: a spiritual soul, a mind able to analyze, decipher and comprehend the world we live in, an emotional heart, a sensory body and a live connection with the world.

The light from within shines when we remove the distractions and find ourselves in the flow. The synchronized combination of mind/heart and soul is expressed when one is in a state of flow. When your being is in a state of internal coherence, the full human expression comes naturally. I found myself in the flow when I write. It is an activity that comes to me naturally and effortlessly to the point that the words simply align themselves in a creative cohesion.

The knowledge of the soul is mysterious and can be compared to an ethereal substance that is released when clarity, purpose, meaning and guidance are sought from within. And this connection with the divine is inherent as the scriptures confirm that God put within us of His spirit. Thus, the spiritual flame is the lighthouse of our human experience.

The soul is nourished with divine communication, scriptural knowledge, communion with nature, mindfulness and awareness of God's existence.

My experience with faith started when I sincerely sought God and step-by-step, I was guided through a path of discovery.

Interestingly enough, since primal and ancient civilizations, the quest for spirituality dealt with the meaning of life, the after death and the soul journey.

The spiritual enlightenment is what brings completion to the human beings, enabling them to reach the highest level of human consciousness.

Now, what are the steps towards this spiritual discovery and how to nurture the divine within us?

It starts with self-awareness, reflection, education, contemplation and deductive reasoning. Faith brings answers to those metaphysical questions that the philosophers started asking. The wonders of creation, life and death and the construction of the universe are some of the signs that indicate the presence of a Higher Entity enabling the harmonization and functionality of all that exists.

I am who I am – Ehyeh Asher Ehyeh – the God who brings things into being. אֶהְיֶה אֲשֶׁר אֶהְיֶה

YHWH – the Tetragrammaton - Yahwey Asher Yahway - the One that brings into existence everything that exists. יהוה

Al Hayy Al Qayyum – the greatest name - the ever living, the one who sustains and protects all that exists.
الْحَيُّ الْقَيُّومُ

Knowledge of the divine entity is what humans crave and God's light is shone through the ages, across time and space. Humans have always developed this belief in the ultimate truth of His existence. When this truth is found, everything makes sense and everything aligns. And it is the full cohesion of mind, body and soul that allows us to access this divine dimension of completion.

3- The psyche

I have to dedicate a portion of my writing to talk about the psyche because it has a huge impact on our day-to-day life.

Understanding how the mind works is key to unlock the ins and outs of who we are because our mind is affected by all the elements that comprise it.

It is true that everything that you have come in contact with has had an impact and knowing that enables a clearer assessment of the self.

It all starts from your lineage, your ancestry, your genetic code, your parents, your family, your childhood, your education, your culture, your environment, your friends, your social network, etc. And this is what has created the blueprint of your paradigms.

One cannot deny the effect of the psyche on daily life and understanding how the background of it impacts our beliefs, actions and behaviors. Even more in modern times, the recent Covid pandemic has literally altered the collective consciousness of humans who have experienced fear, confusion and a general feeling of uneasiness. So nowadays, mental health has never been so important. Notwithstanding all the childhood memories and traumas that one has acquired in the course of experiencing life.

The mind has memories lodged in the depths of the subconscious and the body also has a cellular memory. This fact is scientifically proven with those amazing stories of heart transplants that caused patients to display new behavioral changes.

Interestingly enough, the cleansing and healing of mind, body and spirit are inherent teachings of the scriptures.

The subconscious mind is built for instinctive primal survival and the library of knowledge that composes it is unique to each individual's experience. So, the blueprints of one's mind would have formed those beliefs and acquired behaviors that make you who you are.

To affect the programming of the subconscious, there are known methods through hypnosis, subliminal messages, alpha/theta waves programming, NLP, etc. Obviously, mind control is not something to be taken lightly although we all know that some entities study this in-depth and more... hmm... This is another topic!

Considering that the subconscious mind affects our present reality, I research my inner state and ponder about my childhood and past experiences to make sure that I don't carry any unresolved traumas or relationships that would affect me now.

Where would it begin?

The first bond is the womb link where the baby brain is created at a cellular level and this is why motherly bond, parenthood and maintaining the ties of kinship are scriptural commands. Parental nurturing can be compared to the Godly connection with the functions of giving life, loving, rearing, educating, etc.

Therefore, it is essential to ensure that your relationship with your parents, biological/non-biological, is embedded with love, gratefulness, respect and consideration, regardless of their flaws. Parents are not perfect beings and they always thrive to do their best and carry out their responsibilities according to how they have been raised themselves or in their own ways.

This is why faith recommends maintaining a good relationship between children and parents, because not only is it dutiful, but is also an essential aspect of one person's well-being, as well as a divine blessing.

It is worth noting that the reference to the terrestrial resources is known to be Mother Nature and the divine figure in the Torah and the Bible is the Father. In the knowledge of human consciousness and the cycle of life, parents represent an essential element of the psyche.

Then, I look at my family ties and ensure that nothing is broken and love strengthens those blood bonds of kinship, because God is Love. Thus, I owe it, to my parents and to my family, to feel towards them a loving connection.

Then, I examine past traumas of my life that I may have brought on myself, directly or not, and the impact of others in my life. And I bring in the quality of forgiveness to ensure that my feelings towards others is as I would expect God to be towards me.

Forgiveness is a trauma healer.

It starts with forgiving yourself and knowing that God's mercy is greater meaning that we should be merciful ourselves. Forgive yourself for what happened in your past and open a new page.

When one decides to forgive, it releases the shackles of bondage and cleanses the heart. And obviously, we all hurt people, consciously or not, through words, beliefs or actions and I forgive others because I know that I am not flawless myself. Accepting the humanity of others enables the grand gesture of forgiveness.

Obviously, if a person has been unlawfully wronged and hurt, there are means of compensation and rectification when it is related to their rights. The scriptures mention those situations of wars, battles where retaliation and self-defense are appropriate. The answer to a situation is dependent on the context and the depth to which a person has been wronged. And most answers are found in the scriptures with the elements in context. The reality is that forgiveness has the extra dimension of freeing yourself. And I leave the enemies to God, because Karma has a strange way of coming back at you one way or another. This is my perspective on healing the mind and purifying the heart.

4- The life cycle

One cannot deny the life cycle.

How the Earth functions is an illustration of the life cycle. Existing living things are created from seedlings, then grow and die and the earth recycles everything.

Life on earth is transitory. Every day, people live and die.

The lifespan of a human being is a reality. Knowing that death happens means that one has to be mentally prepared.

All of a sudden, you hear news about someone you know, an acquaintance or a relative maybe, who passed away and the shock of loss and sadness brings along a flow of reminiscing images; vivid pictures of that person alive and some happy memories to cherish. That person who once lived, loved and shared moments now leaves an empty space to those around.

Of course, we all know about the certainty of death and yet, it is always seems to be a far away idea that floats in the mind. It is only when it happens that one gets reminded of its reality and the perception of this world becomes real.

The eternity of the soul has an appeal, rather than the abrupt ending into nothingness. All those souls that have lived exist somewhere in the realms of damnation or paradise according to the scriptural texts.

The heart knows love in this life and death is a lucid reminder of the spiritual purpose of human existence.

5- Traumas & hardships

Everyone experiences hardships, loss, bereavement, traumas, distress, depression, etc. Life is not linear; it is made of ups and downs and the cycle of experiences can have short or lasting effects.

The signs of someone affected by those emotions would include low energy, fatigue, psychosomatic diseases, mood swings, lack of motivation, neglect, paranoia, gloom, etc. When those signs are present, they are symptoms that the mind is affected and it is essential to seek help and support, from professionals if necessary.

Now, there are levels of traumas and depression, and depending on its depth and roots, a therapy might be required. It is worth noting that it can affect all segments of the population.

Learning to identify your own traumas enable you to recognize the source of it and see the why of a feeling, habit or pattern. There are different types of traumas and they have different impacts depending on its intensity, length and frequency.

Managing traumas starts by obviously identifying the roots of it and knowing the triggers that bring those memories and the people linked to those traumas. Being conscious about it is the first step towards recovery.

Faith has been known to bring hope to fragile minds, as well as medical and psychological support. The acquired emotions have to be released physically and mentally. Taking medicine, talking to someone about it, writing your feelings, keeping a journal, body cleansing are some of the options to better yourself. If those emotions are connected to a relationship, it gets sorted once you have come to term with the roots of it and accepted the ins and outs of the experience.

This is not an easy journey and it requires once again self-awareness and insights to acknowledge the situation and solve the problems.

Time has a way of healing those feelings.

6- Mental health

Our mental health as individuals is very important because it affects others.

When I decide to work on myself to achieve well-being, I help others to do the same. Taking the steps to nurture your mental well being is essential and it requires some conscious insights by cultivating self-awareness.

The psyche is a key element for spiritual development. By sorting out the psychological effect of past issues and traumas in your life, your perception changes and then, you can grow and expand.

Depending on the depth of your life experiences, you or your inner circle will know the type of help you need. For some, therapy might be needed while others can do it themselves.

Depression is a reality and people have had their mental health affected by different factors. For instance, cases of wars, battles, deaths, pandemics, diseases, betrayals, abandonment, violence, toxic people and situations have had an effect of the mental health of the community. The first step towards recovery is to perceive the state of your mental health and seek help if necessary.

Obviously, it takes efforts to look within, to become aware, to acknowledge cause and consequence, to take responsibility and to action changes.

I understand my human frailty and I work on it.

I see my divine greatness and I get inspired by it.

7- Self-love and self-esteem

Depending on how the baby was nurtured since conception by the mother and the father, patterns and beliefs would have shaped in the early years, when the subconscious was sponging in the environment. At that age, the brain does not filter the information and absorbs the information that is fed. This is why the first stages of conception and baby growth are so important.

A child cared for in a loving environment will display higher levels of confidence than a child brought up in a fragile household. The characters of the parents, the couple relationship and how they interact with the child breed in the sense of self-love and self-esteem.

The results of parents insulting, denigrating, shouting and swearing at their kids will not bring up a healthy mindset. Loving parents are more attuned to the emotional needs of the youth and generate a suitable environment that brings out the best in them.

Therefore, when a person displays low self-esteem or confidence, it shows that there was some prior mistreatment or experiences that created this inner belief.

Life experiences can also affect self-love and self-esteem because it is linked to the perception you have of yourself.

Self-belief is symptomatic and this is why it matters to look at the roots and origin of a belief, pattern or behavior. When this is identified, it is a matter of reconstructing the belief system into a healthier version.

8- Self image

The mental well-being is also found on one's own perception of self.

What is my self-image?

Do I love myself?

Have I accepted myself?

Do I deem myself worthy?

The answer is that in God's eyes, we are unique creatures and His door is always opened. It is a door of healing, love, joy, abundance and greatness.

So, I choose to love myself, not in a narcissistic way, but in a healthy way. I cherish the mind, soul and body that God has entrusted me with. I love myself with both my flaws and qualities. And I forgive myself for my past, present and future, the same way I expect God to forgive me.

The knowledge that God created us uniquely different with a set of skills, a thinking brain, a beautiful and emotional heart, a body that experiences sensations in the framework of a 3D reality is absolutely wonderful.

Love is a powerful force of good that moves the world.

Traumatic experiences might affect the perception of who you are and this is why developing self-love has a healing impact. When I practice this action of loving myself, it has an immediate impact on my well-being and how I treat myself. In addition to that, how can you expect others to love you without experiencing it yourself? Self-love attracts love.

Love is the source of self-care. Deciding to love yourself means that you are appreciating the divine within you. And this breeds self-esteem and self-worth; having a deep-rooted sense of belonging to the divine Kingdom and knowing that we are worthy in God's eyes to experience life on Earth with all His countless blessings that we cannot even fathom.

Feeding the soul with faith and spirituality, cultivating the mind with beneficial knowledge, looking after our body with nutritional food and exercise are well-known concepts. It is the action of applying our knowledge that makes the difference. We have to remind ourselves about the why of our existence and apply knowledge into action because of what life throws at us. We take the hits and we love ourselves because in fact, life is a test of strength, lessons to learn, wisdom to acquire in order for us to become the best versions of ourselves.

When we acknowledge our depth, our confidence soars to new levels. We are unique spiritual beings living a human experience and how great is that!

CHAPTER II – STRIVING

1- Striving

Life is about striving.

Every day, you strive to be better.

And each moment can take you to the better version of yourself.

Making constant and regular efforts in your life to achieve your goals and purpose is what make life worthwhile.

Faith teaches rituals, routines, behaviors, good character, etc.

I pray every day to nurture a connection with God.
I eat healthily to energize myself with the right food and drink.
I exercise for optimal physical fitness.
I study for mental strength, discipline, actionable and beneficial knowledge.
I work to contribute to society.

I manage my finances responsibly.

I raise a family and build a legacy.

I am in a loving relationship.

I look after my ties of kinship and my inner circle.

I have a greater purpose and contribute to the world.

And I take responsibility for all areas of my life.

Every thought, intention, decision and action matter and this is striving.

When I decide to work on myself to achieve well-being, I help others to do the same.

Life is filled with experiences. We exist to navigate through the waves of life by steering the boat in the right direction. When doing so, we constantly strive to better ourselves through education, networking, friendship, family, behaviors, beliefs, intentions and actions.

Therefore, there is a constant need to reevaluate ourselves and check the state of mind, body and soul.

It is interesting to note that we can be so focused about growing certain areas of our lives, and yet, we are also responsible for developing good character, good habits, worthy values, purifying our intentions, taking the right course of actions to become good and strive for goodness. It is a continual battle of the mind between evil and good. If one strays, then the return to God is what matters.

Perfection is sought while practicing excellence is an art.

Faith is about elevating the soul to divine consciousness; the divine energy gives us such strength and the will to achieve.

2- Overcoming fear

Everyone experiences fear.

What do you fear?
Why do you experience this fear?
How do you intend to face your fears?

It is not about the existence of fear, it is how you deal with it.

What is your approach when you have fear, do you brave it?

Courage is to have the strength to acknowledge the fear and do it anyway. The answer to fear is to display bravery.

For example, public speaking is a tough challenge for most people. How do you solve it? Learn, train, try, make errors, speak until you are comfortable doing it.

It is also important to find what is the root of the fear. Specifically, in the case of phobias, it is usually based on prior experiences that have triggered the phobia. Kids are fearless until they experience it.

Anticipating the worst- and best-case scenario enables us to have a better grasp of a situation.

Practice makes perfect, the more we face or fears, the better we become in our personal growth.

3- Handling expectations

In most cases, disappointments are linked to expectations. Many times, I was disappointed by people because I expected them to think like me. In fact, people are different, they have different values, beliefs, attitudes and behaviors. Understanding that the world is made of plural mindsets, wants and values; I now acknowledge that difference.

Expectations are based on subjective perceptions. And the best way to manage expectations is by clarity and dialogue when it involves people and relationships.

As a parent for instance, you instill in your children the type of behavior you expect from them by giving teachings and instructions. These are reasonable expectations.

When interacting with others and whatever the relationship, communication is the key word for managing expectations.

In terms of self, it is good to have high expectations of yourself. Raising your standards when it relates to self-image, character and being, goals and vision. When you do so, you inspire others to do the same and you attract like-minded people.

4- Managing distractions

As technology has advanced, distractions have multiplied and our attention span is shorter than before, as our brain becomes accustomed to fast information.

Communications, purchases and transactions are now made in a click. It is certainly practical as it enables growth and development.

Marketing and advertising agencies have utilized the online platform to promote products based on customer profiling. While watching a video, pop-ups and ads will appear enticing you to click to another site and capture your attention.

The entertainment, gaming, recreational, retail and e-commerce industries are massive and our attention is constantly diverted to novelties. What is the next best thing? Which innovative discovery is trending?

The worldwide web, instant communications, online dating, software apps, social media have changed people's lifestyles. It is easy to get carried away, surfing and browsing the internet for hours, so the challenge is to manage where our attention goes.

Now what really matters is to be focused in your vision, goals and objectives. We can concentrate better when we commit to the task at hand.

5- Stress management

Stress is a common complaint.

We all experience stress.

Stress is linked to how we perceive ourselves and our situation and it requires sometimes to think out of the box to see it from a different perspective.

What matters is how we manage stress by taking responsibility for our life. Note that positive stress can be a fuel for proactive action.

When one is overwhelmed and stressed, life can be difficult. This is why stress management, particularly in these modern times, is a skill to learn.

To overcome stress, there are some techniques such as:
-time management
-delegating tasks
-prioritizing activities
-practicing self-care
-sports
-meditation and relaxation
-mindfulness
-spirituality

6 - Filtering information

While information has been greatly facilitated by technology, information overload is the downside of it.

Therefore, the rise of information, communication and technology at a global level, means that it is important to be selective in what you feed your mind with.

The internet has brought so much knowledge to our fingertips that learning and educating oneself has never been so easy. This is why the mind can greatly benefit from knowledge acquisition by learning to distinguish the type of information that matters for its growth and development.

Information is to the brain what food is to the body.

The mind trains, evolves and grows by acquiring knowledge, processing it, analyzing it, reasoning, making deductions, innovating and generating new data. The interaction of the neurons and the brain activity create new neural links and spark creativity.

CHAPTER III – THE INNER WORK

1- Building self-confidence

Self-confidence is linked to being aware of who we are and acknowledge our capabilities, skills, knowledge and expertise to utilize them for the benefit of humanity.

Self-confidence is a reflection of self-image. It doesn't mean that one doesn't go through periods of doubts, sadness or depression, but rather than the inner belief is so strong that it stands against everything that doesn't align with its constructed values.

Therefore, self-confidence is the acknowledgment of the self in harmony with itself and the collective consciousness.

Being confident, not arrogant, enables us to explore those unique gifts, strengths, capabilities and potential that are within. Taking the steps to go further, to rely on our God's given abilities and fulfill our purpose on earth.

Finding ourselves in God enable us to take guidance from the intrinsic spiritual light of goodness and greatness to construct a world that is aligned with the collective aspiration.

Suffering is usually a symbol of imbalance or a test. God created us to thrive in this life and how can one not thrive while connected to the source of everything?

In God's name, I live, I love and I experience the gift of life that we have on earth.

It is important to build the confidence to overcome hardships, set-backs and negative thoughts and attitudes from ourselves and others.

We are sometimes our own enemies is a common phrase, in the sense that within the human beings, there are capabilities for evil and good, for harm and righteousness, for sadness and joy, for depression and well-being, etc. So, this is why self-awareness allows us to identify the signs that can trigger our behaviors.

In order to grow self-confidence, it is essential to build yourself in all aspects and project this self-image of the confident You that you want to become. Believe in it and take the steps. Learn, grow and develop yourself until you become that person, the best version of yourself.

What is the best You that you want to become?

Breathe in and integrate this image, the attitude, the behavior, the life, the career, the speech, the energy and this new vision of You will propel you forward to become it.

Surround yourself with the right people that push you forward, uplift you, feed you with this positive image, motivate you to grow, energize you, challenge you to grow out of your comfort zone and build confidence in you.

Self-confidence is born from the inner work and is strengthened by your inner circle and your environment.

2- Self-care

As a mum, I can tell you that we are built in to take care and nurture. And it is only normal that self-care should be part of your daily routine.

Why is it important? Because it is only by taking care of yourself that you can take care of others.

So, self-care matters.

For women, it manifests externally through skin care routines, hygiene, beautification, fashion, nurturing their femininity and in men, with hygiene, grooming and caring for their masculine traits. Internally, it is looking after the inner state of being.

Since ancient civilizations, self-care and beautification have been part an essential part of the human culture, as exemplified by water cleansing, fragrance soaps, essential oils, perfume and incense, earth mineral coloring and make up, gems and jewelry, fabric crafts and cultural clothing adapted to the weather and the environment.

Dedicating a portion of your time to look after yourself, mentally and physically, to show yourself in a well-presented manner makes the self beautiful.

Self-care manifests in attending to the mind and body needs and everything that makes us humans.

3- Mind reprogramming

To retrain the mind to have a different perception of the self entails a reprogramming of the subconscious, as it impacts decision making, patterns and behavior. While the conscious mind is more rational and pragmatic, it is still subjective to the compliance of the psyche.

Faith, positive thoughts, the use of affirmations, scripting, acknowledging oneself, constructive knowledge, a support network, uplifting friends and family are some of the tools that help to reestablish a constructive mindset.

There is no doubt that the mind impacts the environment and vice-versa. This is why feeling high vibrations send positive vibes to its surroundings as a ripple effect.

Deciding who you want to become requires reformatting of the subconscious to align it with the conscious mind. This is why it is necessary to do the inner work to achieve a transformational mindset. When the mind is aligned, new beliefs are formed, the momentum is created and the limbs follow up into action.

The conscious mind can be target focused with awareness and concentration. The state of conscious awakening help develop and raise the levels of consciousness. Elevating the energetic vibrations is achieved with the right mindset and perception.

The different levels of consciousness that imprint the human mind are achieved through the subconscious being in line with the elevation of the soul.

4- You are enough!

I don't know where this feeling of not being enough comes from! Early conditioning, traumas, life experiences can bring in the sensation of inadequacy and this is just an error of perception.

You are enough!

You are enough because God created you in the best manner and provided you with everything that you need.

So being enough means that you decide to accept yourself the way you are, love yourself with your flaws and qualities, forgive yourself and others for everything that has happened, assess where you are and acknowledge where you are going.

I am enough because God has chosen me to be among those who believe.

I am enough because I have decided to love myself, to build myself, appreciate who I am, where I am and where I am going.

This is the essential foundation for advancement.

No one can do this on your behalf.

So, decide today that you are enough because you are unique.

5- Uniqueness

We are all created unique human creatures in all aspects of our genetic code, constitution, character and abilities. This is what makes the world interesting, the diversity and the blend in colors, races, genes, lineages, skills, energies, etc. And at the same time, we are all connected. The feeling of separation is nonexistent because of the divine matrix of collective consciousness.

Accepting that people are different is the first step towards understanding one another. This is why it is important to acknowledge who we are, what we stand for and understand that the world perception is subjective to the individuals.

In fact, we tend we tend to connect more with people who are like-minded or similar in values, principles and energies.

There is a human tendency to make comparisons all the time, it does not make sense because everyone has a different journey in their story, life experience, evolution and growth.

There is no need to compare yourself, the richness of an individual lies in its peculiarity and unique completeness.

Therefore, we all have to follow our path towards greatness, well-being and success.

The scriptures provide the criteria for distinctness and it is related to mind and heart cleansing and soul elevation to the divine consciousness.

6. Expressing yourself

God has gifted us with a voice, the ability to express ourselves, in words, in eloquent speech, in creative ways such as the artist, the painter, the sculptor, the dancer, the musician, etc.

We all have this inner gift of speech to inspire, to teach, to educate, to explain, to tell a story, to inform, to persuade, etc. Finding your voice is key for spreading your message to the world.

It is interesting to note that the Word of God is the concept that is taught in the scriptures. Speech, whether oral or written, is what creates beliefs, emotions and teachings.

In the beginning was the Word,
And the Word was with God,
And the Word was God. (Bible, John 1.1)

Whether you have a tendency to be an introvert or an extrovert, it is primordial to speak out and show up in the world.

Find your voice,
Words are powerful,
They can raise emotions,
Awaken souls,
Heal hearts,
Persuade minds,
Inspire people,
Teach lessons,
Strike rhetorically, poetically, rhythmically,
To become an enchanting expression of the creative mind.

7- A new perception

The world is a reflection of our subjective perception.

And this is why I talk a lot about the mind because the psyche is the first step towards reform and transformation.

Imagine what happens if you fill your mind with news, negativity and low energies, it affects your well-being and perception of the world.

What about doing the opposite? Listening to energizing, motivating, uplifting and positive words that transform you in your best self. This would create positive vibes and leave an impact on the world.

I am the sum of my beliefs, actions and behaviors and I have my own perception of reality. I influence collective consciousness, that symbolizes the global sum of individuals' impacts and effects.

When I change my perception of the world, it affects my reality.

When I see the world as divinely blessed, filled with love, joy and abundance, it has a ripple effect on the collective consciousness. And others start to ponder, reflect and want to share this vision.

Do you harm when you love? No, when you love, you support, you help, you collaborate and your world expands to like-minded individuals.

When love fills the heart, creativity ensues, clarity revives, faith overflows and the divine light shines as a healing magnet.

CHAPTER IV – CULTIVATING GREATNESS

1- Being grateful

If I had to teach one important message to incorporate in the daily routine, it would be to instill the mindset of gratefulness, because the feeling of lack is not a divine attribute.

The scriptures teach gratefulness and how can one be not grateful for the countless blessings that are bestowed upon us?

There are always things to be grateful for and this mindset of gratefulness is the basis of growth. One has to be appreciative in the Now to create a great future.

Appreciation of the Now is the foundation of contentment. When you see what is happening in some parts of the world, it puts your own situation into perspective and you realize those things that you might have taken for granted. On this basis, you develop a growth mindset.

How to develop this grateful mindset?

Make a list of all the things that you already have: eyes to see, ears to hear, mouth to speak, limbs to make and move, a will to do, a mind to think and comprehend the world, instant access to knowledge, a home, a family, parents, friends, work and social life, etc. The list is endless!

If every day, we wake up looking at everything that we have, how grateful we would become!

Obviously, materialism in society evaluates richness from wealth and status, while true wealth is a combination of elements that includes an abundant mindset, an attitude of gratefulness and appreciation, lineage and family, wealth and assets, beneficial knowledge, a sound heart, a discerning mind, a noble character, good manners, a meaningful life, an ultimate purpose, contribution to society, etc.

There is a tendency for people to always look at what is lacking and this is not the abundant mentality. So, learning to see what is already there and envisioning what would be is the way forward.

Look around you, your cup is full, you already have everything and when you are grateful, God gives you more. The Lord is magnanimous to His creatures. So, don't get distracted by the external glitz, embrace this feeling of inner completeness and bring it in from the Source, the Kingdom of plenty.

Gratefulness brings contentment and ambition breeds growth.

2- Heart cleansing

We often take care of the visible aspects of our life and we forget to check the state of our spiritual heart.

We all have flaws that can be worked upon.

Bad habits or negative traits can be reformed. For instance, when one feels those bad emotions such as greed, envy, hypocrisy, excess, hatred, rancor, pride, perversion, selfishness, criticism, stinginess, doubt, neglect, laziness, evil thoughts, etc. The way to manage those feelings is to acknowledge that we are humans and challenge yourself to do the opposite.

The way I reform my heart is by acknowledging my flaws and rectifying them. If I have ill feelings towards someone, I distance myself from them and wish them good. If I ever gossip about someone, i praise their good qualities. If I see someone erring, I find them excuses. If I experience jealousy, I remember to wish for others what I wish for myself. If I have a grudge, I search my own self first to see if it is justified, identify what are the causes of it, fix the situation if I can and if not, leave it to God, as the heart is the most precious aspect of a human being and I cherish a clean heart.

I emphasize heart cleansing because keeping negative emotions affect your own well being. By liberating yourself from ill-feelings, you help yourself as well.

It requires inner strength to acknowledge those flaws and counteract them by forcing yourself into the action of doing more good deeds and practicing love, forgiveness, generosity, praise, kindness, humility, empathy, assertiveness, tolerance, cleanliness, truth telling and thus growing into a noble character with good manners.

Healing the heart beautifies the character.

Cultivating a good character and praiseworthy qualities make all the difference. It enhances the person and beautify people relationships. A smile, a thank you note after a meeting, an apology for a delay, a thoughtful gift, gallant gestures, etc. All those little actions and thoughts that make the day even more amazing.

The heart emotions and thoughts translate into words and actions. A good heart speaks good and direct the limbs to good deeds.

The speech is often a mirror of the heart. Good speech inspires, uplifts, teaches and transforms, this is why the scriptures talk about preaching the good word in an eloquent manner.

Interestingly enough, the scriptural teachings are all about transforming the human being into wellness and greatness by reforming the character, purifying the heart, clearing the mind, correcting behaviors and fulfilling responsibilities in order to attain an elevated spiritual station.

3- Purifying intentions

Intentions are the spirit of an action.

When you do something, the value of that action is enhanced by the quality of its intention.

In faith, actions are rewarded according to their intentions so an act intended for the sake of God gets double blessing.

Questioning yourself prior to an act is a good way of keeping accountable for your actions.

I always review my intention prior to doing something and even after. As I want to cultivate a clear conscience, I take accountability for my intentions. I don't intend harm, I wish good for others. When I do something, I review myself as to the why so that I cultivate this great spirit of constructive intentionality.

I emphasize intentions because in most cases, they are conscious decisions, unless the actions are instinctive and spontaneous. Therefore, good actions are beautified by the right intentions.

4- Health and fitness

Physical health is linked to your energy level so it makes sense to be attentive to your health and fitness levels.

There is no doubt that everyone knows about eating healthy and being fit. Beyond the knowledge, it is the daily application that bring results.

Humans are creatures of habits and it entails building efforts by constructing the right set of attitudes.

Creating good food habits and exercising regularly has clear benefits in terms of energy levels and good health.

Taking the time to go outdoors for a brisk walking and regular exercise, in whatever form, is praiseworthy as fitness empowers brain and body. Sports release endorphins to the brain, the 'feel good' factor and build body strength.

Eating fruits and vegetables, prepping a well-balanced plate of food and hydrating with water translate into a healthy body.

Motivating yourself to acquire new habits require some efforts but it achieves physical well being.

5- Beyond the comfort zone

When I think about the comfort zone, I associate it with the subconscious mind. The same way the baby is nurtured in a cocoon of love, care and protection, the subconscious mind is built on a survival mode, ensuring that everything is within the known framework.

Alternatively, growth is achieved by stretching out and experiencing uncharted territories. Pushing the limits of yourself to go the next mile, to do more, to learn, to grow as a person to fulfill your ultimate purpose. It can be compared to the athletic performance; going beyond the physical limits of the body.

Challenging yourself to do a task that you are not comfortable with helps you develop.

To grow out of your comfort zone, you need to expand, expose yourself to coaches and mentors, mix in different social environments, experience trial and error to perfect yourself, plunge into the unknown and this is when you discover the depth of who you are and who you are meant to be.

Networking with people of different cultures, languages and abilities open the mind to greatness. Travel has been known to be a good way to grow yourself and understand others even better.

6- The importance of education

Education is key.

The scriptures mention knowledge repeatedly as the way to elevate the soul to divine consciousness and understand the world.

Among all the living creatures on Earth, the human species has displayed a capacity for knowledge understanding and implementing, thus impacting its evolution.

Modern times have shown a fast-forward technological civilization as the humans have conquered instant and global communication, fast transportation, scientific research and development and even spatial travel. Interestingly enough, this technological evolution hasn't equated to perfect living conditions for the human beings on Earth. This means that modern advancement is in fact complementary to spiritual, mental and physical well being.

Knowledge is a lifelong commitment and learning is intrinsic, scriptural, conceptual, sensorial, experimental and interactional. We learn from own story and the experience of others. We learn from our parents, educational background, environment and scholars, mentors, coaches and leaders.

As learners, we have different abilities. The three categories are visual, auditory and kinaesthetic types of learning. Obviously, depending on one's craft and abilities, the teaching model can be adapted. Technical work is a more hands-on approach than academic literature!

Depending on your learning type, some material might be more adapted. Texts and videos for visual learners, podcasts and audio books for auditory ones and hands-on experimentation for the kinaesthetic. And it might be that mixing the learning modes is an option to optimize your understanding.

The benefit of technology is that the internet has given an unlimited source of knowledge and access to information from across the world. Whatever you want to learn can be achieved. And everything can be learnt. A baby born knows little until the brain is infused and stimulated by its environment.

7- Seeds of greatness

You plant the seeds of greatness when you decide that you want to be the best version of yourself. Notwithstanding the opinions of others and allowing yourself to be great. Being great is to become who you are meant to be cultivating those qualities and building the mindset for it.

What does the great version of yourself look like?
How does it feel?

Building the best version of yourself requires a will, an emotional trigger, an expansion mindset and educating yourself to nurture your strengths and grow into greatness.

Greatness brings an overflow of love, abundance, joy, positive vibes and constructive endeavors.

Greatness in terms of energy is about vibrating at a peak level of performance.

High vibrational beings emit positive vibes and display magnetic charisma. When the human being is aligned in its mind, body and soul with a constructive mindset and a high energy level, it becomes a source of light and inspiration.

Decide today to be extraordinary!

CHAPTER IV- MINDFULNESS

1- Breathing

The first thing that a baby born does is breathing. The baby breathes from its abdomen. The diaphragmatic breathing is common in babies and children and as adults grow, the breathing becomes shallow and chesty.

Interestingly enough, meditation practices teach breathing techniques. For the simple reason that breathing is what brings the oxygen to the brain and body cells.

When one exercises, moderately or intensely, whether stretching, endurance or interval training, the breathing is affected and there are variations in the heart rate.

Even in singing, reciting and speaking, one exercises breathing, taking pauses when reading long sentences for example. When one is upset, angry, excited or in panic, the breathing accelerates and shortens. And when one is relaxing, the breathing becomes longer and deeper.

Breathing brings in the air that is in the atmosphere and the body releases CO_2 and this air flow connects all of us together. We breathe in harmony with the rhythmical terrestrial waves.

Going back to basic human functioning is a good way to reset mind and body. So breathing is connected to mindfulness, oxygenation and well-being.

2- Thoughts awareness

Can you stop your stream of thoughts? When you do that, you bring awareness to your mind.

I read a while ago about some methods to empty the mind and disrupt the stream of thoughts. It can be by asking your mind questions such as: "What is the color of my thought?"

Another method is to distance yourself from the thought, like an observer and acknowledge it passing through.

Thousands of thoughts fill our mind on a daily basis and they can be imaginative or linked to past, present or future. A thought is a creative imprint.

It is important to cultivate awareness of your thoughts so that you are able to distinguish when negative thoughts come and dismiss them.

Decide which thoughts you want to cultivate by practicing positive affirmations and auto-suggestion.

3- Cultivating mindfulness

Mindfulness is about being present. In fact, we always have to remind ourselves that the only moment that we have is Now. Our mind constantly wanders between past and future thoughts, while the reality is in the present.

Attending to the now is to gather mind, body and soul in alignment. This is when you become aware and mindful.

Right now is where I am alive.
Right now is when I think, do and act.
Now is the right moment.

There is no yesterday, no tomorrow except in your mind. The now is the eternity of the moment.

To feel the now requires you to become sensorially aware of your movements in the space/time moment.

I bring myself to the now by acknowledging my body presence in the space I am in, breathing in the environment and focusing the mind on the activity.

Mindfulness is about being fully present in the moment.

4- Learning to trust your instincts

Within the human body, there is a source of intrinsic knowledge, a connection to the infinite.

This intrinsic knowledge in humans allow them to detect energies, situations and people; knowing how to trust your gut feeling, the inner knowing that gives you certainty.

Humans have a synergy with Earth when they develop sensory awareness and deepen their connection with the natural environment.

There is synchronicity within the body when one becomes attuned to cellular body talk. The body expresses signals, symptoms, healing and intuitive knowledge. There are interesting expressions such as gut feeling, heartfelt knowledge and emotions, etc. that symbolize the inner energetic guidance compass.

Intuition is that perceived understanding, a feeling, a know-how that directs you away or towards certain people. It could be the warning of a situation, readable signs, an influence in decision making that is often confirmed in the reality.

Depending on the level of awareness, intuition is that inner voice that provides information. It cannot be explained, it is simply felt. The something that tells you who or what and an inspiration that tells you what isn't for you and what befits you.

Interestingly enough, each time I dismissed that inner voice, I was proven wrong. Meaning that I learnt to trust myself in the decision making and/or the choice of interactions.

5- Feeling the universe

With the hustle of life, we sometimes forget to see what is in front of us. The environment we live in is absolutely wonderful. Our sensory body has the ability to perceive a 3D reality that is rich in greatness and wonders.

Hearing the birds in the morning, feeling the wind in your face, taking a stroll in nature pathways, looking at the azure sky and traveling clouds are some precious moments that create the awareness that we belong to something greater than ourselves.

This translates into actions such as contemplating and observing the universe, growing an acute sensing of the environment we live in and acknowledging that our feet walk on magnetic earth whilst our head reaches heavens.

The life wonders in nature are a symbolic representation of the variety of living things. Within the same species, millions of different types of design, color, size that beautifies the environment we live in. Therefore, multiplicity and diversity make the world interesting.

At a cosmic level, contemplating the sky view of the Earth, observing the movements of the planets, pondering upon the billions of galaxies bring awareness to the galactic dimension we belong to.

How can we not be in awe of the universe we live in?

This observation makes one wonder about how this reality came to be and the purpose of the human species living on Earth. It calls for metaphysical questions, scientific research and divine presence.

6. Cleansing rituals

There are many cleansing rituals that are known across philosophies and creeds.

Cleansing symbolizes the ritual of purification and it includes cleanliness of the mind, body, soul and environment.

It is interesting to note that water cleansing is a ritual across many religious beliefs, whether through ablutions, water immersion, washing rituals, etc. as a token of purification.

Water symbolically purifies the body of sins as well as physical hygiene maintenance.

The body is cleansed with water, the mind is cleansed with good thoughts and intentions, the soul is fed with spirituality, the heart is purified with good traits and the overall energy is cleared with regular cleaning of the home and the environment.

Our senses are the door of perception to the world and this is why regular cleansing is essential for enlightenment.

Cleansing has been associating with water purification, enchanting incense, gemstones, positive energy vibes, spiritual chants and scriptural readings.

7. Caring for your environment

Beyond the mind, body and soul, the space we live in is an integral part of our existence. We live and breathe in a space that carries energy, so it is worthwhile cleaning, airing and cleansing the space regularly.

Cleanliness purifies the space and airing brings in new energies. Moving material things in the home revitalizes the flow of energy.

Painting and decorating, changing the furniture arrangement enable design beautification, spatial and visual empowerment whilst renewing the energy.

We spend much of our time indoors or in enclosed spaces. Now, considering the recent pandemic, home has to be made into a nurturing space.

Your environment should therefore reflect who you are and your mindset. Obviously, depending on your circumstances, time, budget, frame of mind, occupants, where you live will be made a home. A home is a place of nurturing, love, growth where you recharge yourself.

It is felt most when you travel and you are happy to return home.

8- Decluttering

Decluttering is a good way to create space, cleanse energy and bring in the new. In the course of our life, we accumulate so many material things that decluttering is a good habit to have.

Sorting out your things on a regular basis brings clarity to the mind.

Clutter is actually a mindset, in the sense that some people would have tendencies to either hoard things, be moderate or be minimalist. When it is excessive, clutter can also be the symptom of psychological issues. Hoarders tend to associate matter with emotions. This is why some people find it easier to let go of things and buy new stuff compared to others.

A cluttered home can indicate a lack of storage/space, disorganization or creativity. A tidy and clean home reflects clarity, adequacy of storage and good organization.

As we get attached to things and some items may hold a sentimental value, it is normal to appreciate what we have. In modern societies, consumption and materialism are cultural trends. Wealth is often associated to an accumulation of material belongings, luxurious furnishings, modern appliances, tastefully designed decor, acres of lands and properties.

CHAPTER V- LOVE

1- Feeling love

It is when you develop the love within yourself that you can express the love towards others.

As you feel God's love and grace on you, parents and family love, the bond of friendship, social interactions and your own appreciation of who you are, you become loveable.

Within the depth of your heart, you find this intrinsic well of emotions. When mutually shared, the sensation of loving and being loved is powerful.

A heart full of love is magnetic, inspiring and spreads good vibes in its environment.

God is love. Self-love breeds love and loving relationships beautify the life of this world.

In a world where materialism has become the trend, love is the force that awakens hearts and spirits to the highest level of being.

2- Showing love

Do I have to say that? Yes indeed!

How many times do you say I love you?
Do you show love in words and in actions?
Do you offer gifts to one another?
Do you tend to your loved ones' emotional needs?

Love is heartfelt,
An exchange of feelings,
That beautifies what it touches,
Enhancing the beauty of the universe,
As lovers build and nurture that edifice,
Growing and planting seeds of emotions,
In a bond of human connection,

Bursting love is a synergy of energies,
A meaningful word in concept,
A physical verb in actions,
A spiritual soul in creation,
And sentiments in motion.

Love is a mode of expression that is nurtured with sweet words, attentive gestures, acts of kindness, thoughtful messages and actions that emphasize its depth.

Love can be expressed in a smile, in a conversation, in gallantry, in grand gestures, when opening a door, in humanitarian acts, etc.

Artists are often inspired by love and it shows in their masterpieces.

Artists are admirable and transform speech and matter into magnificent monuments, aesthetic design, intricately detailed craft, exquisite paintings, state of the art buildings, iconic songs and tunes, enchanting poetry, imaginative texts, theatrical plays, inspiring movies etc.

3- Relationship

I thought to dedicate some aspects of my writing to the topic of relationships.

The choice of partner is a big part in your life commitment and not a decision to be taken lightly. Yet, there are so many stories of ill-fitted couples, while the couple unit is the first unit of the family tree and the root of society.

When faced with love commitment, the first step is to identify who you are as a person, where you want to be and what are your must-have criteria.

What matters to you most?
Have you already envisioned your ideal partner?
Do you see yourself having a future together?

In a long-term relationship, after the 'honeymoon' period, it is a journey of discovery. Living with another being means that two individuals are sharing commitment and the constant interaction on a day-to-day basis can cause friction and/or fusion. Habits, character compatibility, communication, trust, feelings, physical synergy, values and beliefs, goals and objectives are all part of the mix.

Selecting your relationship partner or spouse is important because of its implications, such as planning children, etc. Knowing what befits you, having a clear vision of who you are and what person you can relate to, is determinant to your future. This is why it is essential to choose according to your selected criteria as everyone has different wants.

The more you know yourself, the more you know what will work for you. No one can do that on your behalf. Obviously, parents/family can influence the partner selection for their young adults. And as adults, it is a different matter altogether, you take the responsibility of relationship making.

From the relationship building, the family ties emerge. Which family unit are you building?

Relationship is linked to couple bonding and family unit; the first links of society build a community. When the foundation of a relationship is strong, its fruits in children, family ties and societal construct are positive. Healthy mindsets, positive relationships and a constructive family circle create an expansive unity of wellness within society.

4. Inner Circle

What makes your inner circle?

The choice of relationships is essential for your well-being. While family is dictated by lineage and biological descent, who you hang out with is your own decision.

Friendship is usually motivated by like-mindedness, compatibility, positive interaction, reliance, trust and communication.

In personal development, the choice of mentors has an impact on the growth of the individual. Selecting experts in their field is essential to optimize the learning process. The right coach will positively influence the development of the mentee.

The circle of influence are all the people that you are in interaction with and there is mutual benefit in having a constructive network in the field of business and socialization.

The inner circle influences an individual's growth and development and impacts its societal impact.

5.What is your impact on the world?

Knowing your mission, the why of you being on Earth is a question to ask yourself.

Who are you?

What are your beliefs and values?

What are you here to accomplish?

What are the goals you want to achieve?

What is your vision for the future?

How do you imagine the best version of yourself?

To answer those questions, you would need to identify your characteristics, your capabilities and how to awaken your potential into realization. This is why knowing and educating yourself, being selective about your inner circle, transforming yourself internally in order to accomplish what you are meant to be are what matters.

Making those decisions, taking those steps, internalizing your vision until it becomes so real that you bring it into fruition.

6. Visualization process

The visualization process relates to integrating your goals, your objectives and your future perception of yourself into something that is already accomplished. Meaning that the result is not perceived as sought but already there.

Visualization is more than a mere vision, it means feeling, internalizing and instilling energy into the thought of what is to be accomplished.

What fuels manifestation is the emotional energy that is created when you believe in yourself and your vision.

When you are impregnated with your vision, your thoughts, acts and behaviors are transformed. You are it. Your entire being is changed. You have a higher grasp of the thought process; you are committed to realization and you take action towards that vision.

Therefore, manifestation is the result of visualization, emotional empowerment and action steps that translate into a new reality.

7. The path of happiness

Happiness is a mindset.

Contentment equates to appreciating the blessings that you have and it results in gratitude.

The source of happiness can be spiritual. Faith brings hope. Hope means that there is always light at the end of the tunnel. Divine grace is light.

Happiness can be moments of joy.

When good things happen, it is delightful. Depending on the individual, the reason for rejoicing can vary. Good news, an exam passed, a wedding, a baby born, a successful venture, an achievement and material fortune are some of the blessings of this life.

Happiness also manifests in times of mindfulness when mind, soul and body are aligned in the moment. The anxiety of past and future disappear when one is present.

Developing a positive mindset, cheerfulness, love, abundance, self-realization leads to well being.

And achieving well being brings delight.

8. Breeding success

Success means different things to different people.

What does success mean to you?
What is your vision of success?
What is the successful version of you?

Success is achieved with the right mindset,
The mindset of accomplishment and progress,
Progressing into who you want to become,
Becoming the 'who to be' with the small wins,
Wins that cumulate into a list of accomplishments,
Accomplishments that you can praise yourself for,
And thus program your mind into a winning mode.

Understanding that failures and setbacks are the step stones to success The road to triumph is winding with hits and rocks. This is why being persistent is an essential quality for success.

Falling, failing and standing up again and again until you reach your destination.

Persistence to believe in your vision and conquering obstacles create achievements.

Achievements bring success realization.

Success realization is to stand at the top of the mountain that you have handbuilt with your own desired accomplishments.

CONCLUSION

In this book, we have covered the milestones of mental conditioning, psyche, spiritual empowerment, character building as well as mind, body and soul alignment.

The purpose of this book is to bring an awareness of what humans are made of; understand the mind to create the foundation for reform and transformation.

Self-realization is a journey that incorporates all the steps that one takes to comprehend oneself and the world we live in.

Achieving overall well-being and success equates to:

-elevating your soul spiritually,

-building your mindset,

-educating yourself,

-cleansing your heart,

-building physical strength,

-strengthening family bonds,

-establishing social construct,

-creating financial wealth,

-growing your career,

-investing in societal contribution,

and spreading energetic, healing and positive vibes in the world with a spirit of joy, love, abundance and happiness.

We are all connected and impact one another.

By healing yourself, you bring healing to others and inspire constructively.

Start this journey of healing and become extraordinary!

ABOUT THE AUTHOR

Chahrazade Belamine is a university postgraduate with ten years professional expertise in sales, marketing and business growth within startups and SMEs. She is currently working on some entrepreneurial projects.

Equipped with an inquisitive and spiritual mind, she has sought religious knowledge for more than 20 years to understand the scriptures and the divine message. She speaks several languages and has written in both English and French. She has a keen interest in faith, personal development and business growth.

Her other books available on Amazon:
- Plug-in tips for business start-ups (business book)
- The poetic prose of life rose (poetry)
- Atheism+logic=faith (spirituality) EN/FR
- Jesus in the Divine Kingdom (spirituality) EN/FR
- The inspired ray of Islam (spirituality) EN/FR
- Reflections on Islamic scripture (spirituality) EN/FR
- A synopsis of Islamic concepts (spirituality) EN/FR
- Q&A in light of the Quran (spirituality) EN/FR

Printed in Great Britain
by Amazon